GW00854650

Crows' Books

Anne McDonald

Seabhac

Publishing

Dublin, Ireland

Front cover artwork "Autumn Glory" by Anne McDonald

© 2020 Seabhac Publishing

All rights reserved.

For Larry,
Sinéad & Jack

There have been many people who have helped in the creation of this collection. To everyone that offered encouragement, support, space for me to share the poems, suggestions, edits and enthusiasm, I owe a sincere thank you.

To my editor and all the team at Seabhac who believed in this collection from the start, thank you for sticking with me during the strangest of years.

Anne McDonald

December 2020

Acknowledgments

Some of the poems in this collection first appeared in the following publications, my sincere thanks to the editors of these magazines and journals for giving my poems a space and voice.

https://www.oddmag.co/ (2020) Peggy's Brack *https://poetsdirectory.co.uk/192* (2020) Three Hours Out, *The Blue Nib Online* (2018) Too Soon, *The Blue Nib Issue 41* (2020) Still Birth, Crows' Books, The Letters, Fledglings, *The Strokestown Poetry Anthology 4 (2020)* Whose Coat?, *Live Encounters Poetry & Writing July 2020* Blue Bells and High Horses, Harold in the Hospice, Peggy's Brack, As it was in the beginning, *Live Encounters 11th Anniversary Edition Pendemic.ie (2020)* One Piece Missing. *Boyne Berries Covid Issue (2020)* Precious Treasure. *Women's Work Anthology Vol 1*, (1990/92) Jax.

Contents

Introduction by Muddy D Norman

Anne McDonald's debut collection Crows' Books is a striking narrative which takes ordinary life and turns it extraordinary. From the heart-breaking "Whose Coat?" to the hilarious "Spatchcock Chicken" and through all the poems in between, Anne takes you on a journey of self discovery where you learn to laugh at your self and cry without shame.

With her characteristically adventurous and yet totally relaxed approach, Anne's poetry is full of optimism and love. In this powerful new collection you can hear the poet laugh just as loudly as she weeps.

Muddy D Norman
"Songs from the Worn Hole" 2012, reprinted 2016
"Whalebones" 2019

Muddy D Norman in conversation with Anne McDonald

MDN How did you come to write poetry ?

I have written poetry for as long as I can remember and still have some god-awful angst-ridden sonnets from when I was a teenager. In recent years I returned to writing as the world around me changed. I think I use writing as a means of questioning or reflecting on those changes and how they affect me or give me new insights into what other people are experiencing. On a personal level I find I write by looking back at incidents or memories and learning through the poems that evolve that my perception of events was not the only one at play.

MDN where do you get your inspiration ?

A lot of the time I write to understand things which is where poems like "Whose Coat?" and "Milk in Cartons" come from.

The idea that someone can just go missing is heart-breaking enough, but the grief is compounded by the fact that life, for the families affected, carries on. All the illness, ageing, births, deaths, and accidents will happen anyway, but the pain of people whose loved one has gone missing is compounded by agonizing silence and confusion and no possibility of closure.

Other times I write about the gap in my understanding about an event or something I see that is outside of my cultural upbringing which is where "The Pomegranate Tree" comes from. I love to write about situations that started out as one thing and turned into something quite different like "Tinder Blunder" and I like to write in response to what I see on an everyday basis. I love poems about real people living real lives in a real world that exists outside my front door.

3

I also love to use humour particularly to shine a light on dark places with poems such as "Jax" and "Spatchcock Chicken". To write a poem about the lack of toilet paper in the ladies loo or the indignity of contraception gives me a chance to put words to embarrassing experiences and to use comedy to share that experience which turns out to be universal rather than personal.

I have been really fortunate in recent years to have had the opportunity to perform those pieces at Open Mic nights in Ireland, U.K. and the U.S. and these topics seem to raise a laugh and awareness at the same time, which to me, is the job of a good poem.
Emotion and awareness don't always have to be bleak.

MDN what are the main themes that run throughout the book?

I suppose love, death and loss are common themes for most poets and I also like to write about injustice such as inheritance and patriarchy which is where "The Family Nest" comes from.
I know we have come a long way in Ireland in recent years, but I feel we still have some way to go before we can assume we have genuine inclusion.

Some poems in the collection are social comments on the banality of war, such as "Strip" and "Christmas Bikes, Belfast 1990". Poems like "Excellent Horse Like Lady" are a reaction to the highly ridiculous but unfortunately powerful tyrants we seem to have heading up governments and countries, with access to atomic weapons and in positions of power.

"Guns in Iowa" is a direct reaction to the fact that it is legal in the U.S. state of Iowa for blind people to carry guns.

The innocence of being a child is something I return to a lot in poems such as "Still Birth" or "Crows' Books" where I now understand that it is a very special time to be spared from the real pain of the world that comes with growing up.

Other poems such as "A Good Wife and a Black Truck" are about domestic abuse and the very real decisions people have to make to get to a better place. The poem "Three Hours Out" is based on a real-life event of a cot death and a journey from sea to shore by a crew who didn't know which one of them was going to be affected. It's a poem that resonated with a lot of fishing families and highlights the helplessness of being at sea when a major life event happens.

MDN where did the title "Crows' Books" come from?

My mother told me as a young child that a flock of crows that passed overhead each morning and evening were on their way to and from school. She also said that pine cones were crows schoolbooks and I never found any reason to think otherwise until I got older. For me the title is as much about the innocence of being a child as the imagination that connects us seamlessly to nature before we "grow up" and disconnect.

MDN is there an auto biographical thread running through the book?

I think all poets must write at some point about things they know, feel, did, and do, so in that sense yes there is. Some of the poems shine a light on dark corners of my life and many are written from memories of growing up in the country side in Co. Meath in the '70's. Poems like "Just Desserts" and "Charlie's Tree" are directly connected to instances in time that I remember clearly as a small child.
Many of the poems are written about my mother, about who she was before she had a very serious stroke and how her illness and passing affected those around her.

MDN what do you think the power of poetry is?

I think poetry has the power to make certain that memories and experiences are carved into certainty and therefore cherished.

"Precious Treasure" is about the ability of the humble tin pot to evoke images of a past that may otherwise be lost. Poetry can heal, hear, express, and help us to understand and make special moments we might otherwise lose forever.

MDN how has the pandemic affected you as a poet?

Throughout the months of lockdown and the very surreal experience of our whole way of living being turned on its head, I have found that poets have reached out and connected in a very real and powerful way.

As humans we have to adapt and find new ways to build bridges and share our common, personal, and universal experience.

Open Mic online meetings and events have given a space and voice for poets from all over the world and I have been fortunate to meet, connect, hear and share poetry with people I would never have had the good fortune to meet in person.

If anything, the pandemic has brought home to me the immense value of poetry and the arts in general as a means of healing, expression and recording and articulating a global event that has affected every one of us. It has taught me the value of writing and the very real power of connection.

Three Hours Out

We got the call three hours out to sea
I know that we were thinking all the same
I wonder is it him or is it me?
We had no choice but wait the hours out,
with endless cigarettes and cups of tea,
too harsh for crackling radio to explain,
I hope that it was them and wasn't me.

We made talk so small it meant nothing;
the haul we got, the time we lost the nets,
and when I won the each way bet
but still the time dragged every minute single
out of three excruciating hours, coated in
the sour smell of oilskins mixed with salt.

I listed all the possibles for heartache,
knowing each man counted out the same.
Was the family affected theirs or was it ours?
Strong men rendered naked in the rain.
As we turned for home and braced against the wind

a small crowd gathered silent on the quay,

my head spun somewhere between fear and hope

I wished that it was them and wasn't me.

Our hearts broke for the man whose news it was,

as hands reached down to haul him from the deck,

words whispered on the winds were "cot" and "death."

Feeling glad then sickened with the shame,

but knowing it was not my news to claim,

we got the call three hours out to sea

I wished it wasn't him, that it was me.

Remembering Baby Ryan Minto, born April 18th, 1996 and died in June 1996, aged 9 1/2 weeks.

Rutland Mother

She was born in the belly
of an aching woman,
ripped to stretching
by twenty thousand beltings,
first inhaling rancoured
by the taste of Woodbines.

She grew up in a grass-less
waste of concrete,
living minutes punctuated
by the sunlight,
harsh and violent soundings
feathered with the night-time
prayers of angels.

She coupled by tradition,
and offered up her dreaming
for the scanty wisps of comfort
and security by weekly payment
to an unknown, open, grasping hand.

She mothered with a loving
heedless of the boundaries
but mindful always of the bearings,
always giving
always laying healing palms,
holding in the bleeding heart.

She died today
within her limits,
never knowing cosmopolitan,
—Never needing to.

Too Soon

I trace the branch that spikes the skyline in my head,
black against the orange burnished clouds,
Hitchcock would have painted it in ink.
I think therefore I must exist, I thought,
as light left quietly and wind arrived
to chase gray black clouds across the yellow moon,
it may have been her time
but I disagreed with God,
it was too soon

She died if that's what nature calls it,
in the summer,
but many times before
she died another death
and each a different stroke,
a different set of numbers on a chart
that filled with years and notes and lists
and accumulated fears
and many tears by us, by her, by him,
she grew frail and pale and thin.

In the end she left a shell of what she was,

and though we watched,

there was no burst of blazing light,

no crowd of angels heralding the new arrival

at the gates of heaven or whatever place

she thought she went at night,

just her skin and lips turn slowly white.

Metaphysical insurance of an open window;

to let the soul out

or a draught in,

the fanfare, if there was one, made no sound,

no robin or white feather

on the ground to give the nod or wink.

The branch was pointing upwards

towards the moon,

and even though the harvests counted

fifteen crops since her first big stroke,

as autumn fires call straight to heaven

in a line of curling spears of smoke,

the clock will now forever

tock tick the time

as being too soon,

too soon.

Peggy's Brack

Do you not remember the night you ate the brack?
The night she came home cold and tired from work
and put the kettle on?
It was November and the pump had burst
in the hot press so the house was freezing,
there was very little butter left
and *you* put it on the last slice of brack.

She ran amok;
Threw us all out of the house
we had to go to your house
do you not remember?
Can you not just *pretend*
that you remember about the brack?

She gets confused I know
but to be fair to her it really did happen,
and she gets upset when she gets confused,
Are you *sure* you don't remember?
What would it matter if you played along?

You'll never see her after this.

She might give you a slap or a kiss

depending on how her brain is working on the day.

Would it really kill you to visit for a chat

about when were all teenagers

and she used to work nights

and all the fights and arguments

about dishes in the sink?

Just let her think that you remember.

I'll be with there, you needn't worry

she's not usually violent

only when she gets confused,

but she is right on this score.

We'll be in and out in no time.

I'm sad you don't or won't remember about the brack,

it's all she can remember about you.

Precious Treasure

You see an aluminum steamer,
knocked about by life and dulled from age
no use now for draining pasta
and fit for throwing out a long time since.

I see my mother's hand
chopping cabbage with a saucer
raw from washing dishes
her wedding ring tight on
a swollen finger.

You see a pot with wonky handles
that burns your hand when it gets too hot
and takes up too much room in
the kitchen cupboards.

I see a ham being boiled
for Easter Sunday in our kitchen
when the sunlight makes the steam
a magic carpet.

You see a plastic child's tiara

cheap and chipped and dulled by sunlight,

I see a duchess with dementia,

smiling at her public, being there

but also gone already far from us

on my mother's eighty third birthday

You see old

and broken

tin and plastic,

    I see precious treasure.

Time and Time Again

My mother took an age to walk across
West Street on a Saturday.
She would stop and talk and start again
relaying the same particular story,
whilst we would hop from one foot to another,
freezing cold and gawking into
Tully's misted window.

She brought back packs of Spangles
from shopping trips to Newry on the bus.
Nervous and excited coming home,
relaying close encounters with the army,
bags would burst with bargain packs of OMO.

She wore a purple sweatshirt playing football
with knee high socks to hide her varicosis,
the photo made the Drogheda Independent,
I was ten and she was thirty-seven.

She drove a Honda 50 going to work,

dish-washed into early hours for cash
and tin foil packs of midnight chips and rashers,
a truce to eat by mutual agreement,
because truth be told
we fought like cats and dogs,
and many times I hated her,
I'm damn sure now
she must have hated me.

In later years she doled out labelled parcels
of rhubarb stewed and frozen packed,
lumps of meat and loaves of bread
tin foil plates of "proper" dinners,
visits home were never-ending lucky dips of things
that might be used or useful,
you never knew.

At sixty-two the labels are illegible now,
speech is savaged and depleted,
stature shrunken bent by aneurysm
with frightened eyes and limbs like lead,
I just can't get around it in my head

a more humane condition

would be

to be

dead.

The gale of wind that I remember

giving out and giving,

doing, making, sewing, baking,

going off to Knock or out to swim,

spends hours now in rehabilitation

weeping quietly trying to say "enormous."

Now I would love to walk the length

of West Street on a Saturday,

to stop and hop from one foot to another,

to hear her say the same thing over

again and then again, for the sheer joy of talking.

And I would gladly freeze

in Winter's rain to hear her

tell her stories

time and time

again.

Crows' Books

We watched the flight
of a hundred crows
squawk their way
to the sky-high trees.
My mother said they were
"birds coming home from school."

We rambled on
in the dusk damp woods,
a pine cone lay
under rusty leaves.
My mother laughed and said
"one of the crows has dropped his book."

A pine cone sits
on a rough-hewn desk,
and when I hold it
I am four years old
and hear again my mother's voice,
"there is always crows' books in Pilltown."

Still Birth

Steps of stairs from seven to five
we stood in line on the garden wall,
dressed in gingham, hand made,
handed down, waiting now for hours,
dark hair burnished in the winter sun.
It seemed like years since she had gone
we almost thought we'd never get her back,
but here she was, home.

'Howya Mam,
Where have you been?
What did you get us?'
Our questions clamoured.
'In the hospital' she replied,
her face turned towards the harsh lit kitchen window,
as we all chorused 'why?'

A cardboard suitcase opened on the table,
I saw her touch a pale blue piece of ribbon
and cotton soft, a pale blue baby's bonnet.

Softly I could hear her whisper
'I went to get a baby.'

She must have been a thousand pieces
racked with pain and sore and sad
and patched together dispatched out
to carry on and not look back.
'So where's the baby Mam?'

She held the bonnet to her face,
and broken hearted, spared our pain
but increased hers, when she answered;
'There was only red-haired ones
in the Hospital Shop'.

Wedding Rings

Did you understand us when we said we loved you,
or did you nod your head and smile
just to please us?
Did you mean it when you said that you were
"happy now, not a bother on me, never going home"
knowing Dad was alone by then
and our hearts were breaking when you turned away,
and saved your smiles for strangers?

Did you know how hard we dealt with guilt
knowing "care" was what was best for you,
yet never wanting you to feel abandoned?
And when you answered "everything" for breakfast,
did you know the nursed just guessed
and always gave you porridge?

Did you understand that it was wrong
when your wedding rings was taken from your finger?
When we complained that they were missing
you were made a ward of court, your pension seized

we had to bring receipts and a report
for every pack of tissues or bottle of shampoo?
Five years on I wonder, if, just by chance, that it was
you?

Did you take off the rings yourself and bin them
in a fit of clearing memories and sadness?
Did you understand your hand remained indented,
from the wedding rings, branded with fifty years
of marriage, tears, joy, love and dead babies,
and we are left with "maybes"?

I really hope it *was* your choice, not someone else's
greed and you didn't have to plead
for them to stop
or take some other things.
We learned early on to leave nothing of any value in
your locker.

I really hope you did know all these things,
and that it was you deciding to be free,
not just petty theft of precious wedding rings.

As it was in the Beginning

My mother worried with a wet dishcloth
when we were out too late and ran the risk
of being abducted.
If I close my eyes I can feel the sting of scalded skin
and the faintest smell of mild green Fairy Liquid.

Her mother worried with the smell of seaweed
wet upon her apron
on a mussel bedded shore in Mornington
as she waited for the pilot boat to cross
the bar to safety.
Before that, a mother, a woman I have
no knowledge of whose genes I'm told,
are in my DNA,
worried for a dying flock of children born blue bar one.
Apparently she was a bullock of a woman
for hauling turf.

Now I worry for a 21-year-old,
every inch my 21-year self if I had been a boy.

A party animal who can travel on a whim
and make his way home safely with the dawn.
A bull of a man for carrying blocks
and working fourteen hour shifts
behind a counter pulling pints
 -a charmer with quick mouth.

I worry he will smoke out his twenties
 in a haze of Moroccan black
and Jack Daniels iced and mixed with red
and that one night he will be found dead
 in a ditch somewhere
behind the steering wheel of a crashed car.

But most of all I worry
that he will feel too much,
hurt too much,
go through life an open,
coping wound,
the whole world's worries in his head.
-He actually tells me not to worry.

I worry that he dropped out of the college
he didn't want to go to in the first place
-he smiles a lot from an upturned face.

I've heard it said, at night in bed
you can swap worrying for prayer
if you have any kind of God you could believe in,
apparently it stops anticipatory grieving,
and the thieving of the hours of sleep.

So I keep the gate in the company
of other mothers
and their mother's mothers
standing down the line of years,
fears accumulating in a pile of stones
bleached from generations in the sun,
each one used and borrowed from the next
and handed down
to form eternal monuments.

The Letters

Thoughtlessly I threw your letters
to the fire and went on sorting,
holding and discarding,
the television blared,
I thought of work.

Suddenly,
the pages caught my eye,
they smouldered slowly
as if to fight the flames.

I thought of all
the dreams and hopes
and mainly apologies
those letters held.
And then by chance,
a flame took hold,
and in a moment,
the words were gone
-as you are.

Separate

I learned what love was
when I learned the names
of the mountain flowers.
I felt what love was
when the summer breezes
brushed against my skin.

I found happiness in the wakening
of the morning.
I found all I ever wanted
in you.

I write to you but paper cannot
hold you near.
I think of you but can't be sure
my thoughts are yours.
I pray for you and only hope
that someone listens.

Fledglings

I know you know
you've made a
monumental blunder
I could have told you that in January,
I tried to tell you that in June.
But is it only now,
twelve months later
that it's hit you?

I hope you know the story of the fledgling;
How it faltered for a while
hovered on the quivering branches
wanting to run and hide
within the warmth and comfort
of the family nest.

It waited;
and while it waited,
it lost the downy feathers from its breast
replacing them with multicoloured hues

Silk to touch.

It waited;
While you mulled around
 and beat your head
against the walls
of your monumental blunder.

It faltered for a while
and waited,
until the day came when,
with piercing, searching eyes
it looked into your concave,
saw your thrashing
and subconsciously,
despite itself,
it spread its azure wings
and flew away.

I just hope you know…

A Good Wife and a Black Truck

The spiral was broken when she stopped pretending
and started being honest.
"Is Bill there? He was due on shift at six?"
Annette the supervisor's voice was tentative and low.
 Maribel answered "No. Try the pub.
"Oh" said Annette. "Right so"

"Oh is a good word Annette, thank you for calling.
Sorry if Golden Boy is late for work.
and F.Y.I. the baby is NOT sick,
the dog is NOT in the vets
and all four tires on the car are fully inflated."
Annette waited a moment then said "I see."

"Well, Annette, it was half past three
when he left the house,
it takes fifteen minutes from here to there
so I wouldn't hold out any hopes of him doing a shift
any time soon,
by the way, you should take note

there is a full moon."

The spiral shattered all over the carpet in the hall.

Something lifted a breeze block off her chest.

"One down Artemis" she said to the cocker spaniel

who wagged his tail but looked bewildered.

She had the books,

Feel the Fear,

Change Your Life,

The Best Life with no Strife,

an Absent Wife,

so she knew that sometimes you really do

have to do things afraid.

The long black truck pulled up to the gate

to wait until she had filled it up with five years

worth of a miserable life as a dutiful wife.

She left the washing machine

but took the large painting

of a Japanese peacock

and a miniature gold-faced wind up clock,

bin bags filled with clothes

she later used for rags
to clean the windows in her new place
-a safe space.

The phone rang as she closed the door,
and Artemis carried his own lead to the car.
"Did Bill get paid today do you know?"
"I don't Joe, to be honest, I have to go."

As she drove away behind her life
 in the black truck
driven by Pat the Man,
half truck, half van ,
who could and would shift anything,
she had the sneakiest suspicion
that Golden Boy would never see it coming
and would be genuinely left in shock
up to his narcissistic balls in hock.

Whose Coat?

The coat in the hall is threadbare now,
after 27 years I still stop and stare at it,
willing it to tell me what it knows,
to tell me where you are
or where you went
when you went missing.

Still hung on the same hook,
the same sci-fi book
poking out of the left pocket,
a half empty pack of Amber Leaf
nestled in the right.

At night I touch the frayed edges of the sleeve,
and hear your words above the clang
of metal on the gate
"Don't wait up, I'll be late,"
then you were gone.
The echoes of that metal jangle
still rankle as a last post and chorus

for a lost son.

I will never know if the river was your bed,
if your limbs are still entwined around
some broken scrap of metal,
or pipe of lead dug deep into the mud somewhere.
All I know is that I should have known;
that last note of the metal gate was too late.

You see, I know,
you would never have left the coat.

There are days I want a grave to kneel at,
to dig my fingers into wet clay
and to know your bones and flesh
are sleeping now, at rest.
I always knew the best of days
were still too difficult for you.

Other days I wait and watch the road
where you walked the hundred yards
to get the school bus.

As a child, you thought that cobwebs
were made of silver.
I never told you otherwise.
Now there is only us.

I look to see a blue ridge of gelled hair and the rattle
of a bicycle chain slung low around your waist.
Black eyeliner was "in poor taste for a boy"
according to your father.
He left too
but not like you did.

He sits by day at the window sill,
waiting, wiping fogged up glass
with baited breath and woolen elbows,
his thoughts mixed up with memories
and bits of things,
I sometimes think he knows,
but then he stands and asks
"Is Aidan in yet?"

On his way to bed he touches the coat and tells

me that he never read a science fiction book.

And with a tender good night kiss

he asks me every single night

"Whose coat is this?"

The Family Nest

They always told me I was a surprise,
but I know it was more of
a great big thundering shock.
The rattlings of the bag,
the shake of the sugar sack,
the overlooked afterthought.

They never realized that
it was just as big a shock for me,
catapulted into a blaze
of harsh lights and fights,
bangs and rattles and the low moan of cattle
in the early morning.

A farmer always wants a son
apparently, to pass things on,
land to land, hand to hand.
But he got me, six foot one,
hands no use for cattle prods
or tinkering with tractor engines

but *Top Gun* with a pair of scissors,
and a curling tongs,
sharp as a tack in black with my name
embroidered across my chest in pink.

Mother didn't mind so much
A trim and blow-dry every Friday,
a frothy cappuccino and a massage chair
was a long way from tin buckets,
buttermilk and the smell of day-old slurry.

He said he knew my ilk,
had heard about my kind,
would have no truck with the likes of me,
that when he was a young buck
he carried the plough across his back
at the end of day to give the horse a rest.
He said all sodomites would
have to face God.

Even so, I cut his hair the way he liked this morning,
fixed his tie and shaved his day-old beard

before the coffin lid was closed,
and his onward journey blessed.

It was the least that I could do
before I took my mother home,
and over tea and fingered deeds,
with sniffs of disapproval from
the multi tasking undertaker
at my lack of interest in the spread of hoose,
costs of tillage and the lowering price for beef,
I signed my name in black and definite ink,
and in the blink of a watery solicitor's eye,
I laid the biro down to rest ,
and legally inherited the family nest.

Milk in Cartons

If I lived in Massachusetts
I would see your face
every morning with my cornflakes.
Your date of birth, your height,
your clothes and where you were last seen
on the date of your disappearance.

If I lived in Oklahoma
the man who lives across the hall
could call a toll-free number to report
something he remembered when
he poured a glass of milk to take to bed,
that you had dark hair or were tall.

With dogged perseverance
your face would be for months on end
in Boston when a girl was making pancakes
and if she saw a person just like you
or noticed something out of kilter
the police could filter out what was

relevant to an ongoing open case.

The space around the fat content
would tell me what your last location was
if we were living in Milwaukee.
Anyone who knew anything
would be constantly reminded of who to ring.

But here my milk carton says "Sourced in Ireland."
No one in Dublin or Offaly or Kildare
will remember what you chose to wear
when you left the house or hitchhiked home,
or walked the city streets alone.
No toll-free number or "Have you seen?"
No daily plea for help or reminders
that your eyes are green.

-Just milk
In cartons.

The Glasgow Bus
(Serving Donegal, Belfast, Monaghan, Larne, Glasgow, Departing daily)

Waiting for the stars to shine
to light the pools of glass that frost the path
outside Maggie McGrath's apartment.
Facing down the wind that blows
from Glasgow's inky waters
all the way to Belfast Lough,
sending workers' wages home
and letters back and photographs,
of building sites and dockyards
and potato farms with arms around
each others' shoulders,
of the better life away from all the conflict.

No reproach, just union rates
and dockyard gates are all the same,
no "who's to blame?" for disciplinary actions,
Republican fractions and Loyalist reactions
-raw hands are always red.

Over here the job gets done
with many shades of different skins
and icy winds polish the stars
that hang in strangers' night-sky.
But aching guts long for home
and the bread and butter feel of Ulster,
scalding tea and tatey bread,
redbrick terrace murals
painting history into dreamland
on Ritchie Redmond's gable.
Ulster Fry and Belfast News,
Lambeg drums and Irish dancing.
But use *The Bus Seat Rule* leaving
Letterkenny on a summers evening.

In July the air above the bonfires
rises up and travels east
bringing rhythms of a former life
to the chimney stacks and
high-rise flats of Glasgow.
-Marching is a slow dance walked.

With nervous talk and cans and chatter
one-word nods and shoulder shrugs,
sideways glances and second chances,
we are waiting for the stars to shine
to light the pools that frost the path
outside Maggie McGrath's apartment,
taking turns to pay for comfort,
wanting hope in strangers' arms
-needing home.

Popemobilia

In the Solidarity Museum in Gdansk
the pope-mobile looks as if, by chance,
the pontiff drove it slap into the middle
of the revolution.

Gleaming white against the blood red logo
of the movement, underneath the blackened
yellow dockers helmets on the ceiling,
you get the feeling that Karol Wojtyła
parked it there and just hopped out
to buy his favourite waffles

But that would be a big mistake
because it turns out that the pope-mobile
in the middle of the revolution exhibition
in Gdansk is a fake.

The real mobile has been a pilgrimage for
Marek Adamczyk as he recalls the silent scream,
when Wojtyła toured his homeland in an FSC Star660,

Marek sits proudly for a photo opp
at his desk in his newly constructed
real-mobile museum.

It would seem that Adam
spent his own money and his time
reconstituting the vehicle
from the body shops of lesser Poland
where the communists chopped it up
in 1979.
"This was a labour of love" he said,
"entrance is free."

In Dublin the vehicle that drove
through the Park
is highly visible after dark,
full of roaring stags and hens
now available for hire.
-at three hundred euro an hour.

In the absence of a revolution
in the wake of the Papal tour,

the hope for absolution

in the rubbing of a relic

from an outdated institution

has finally,

in a land of tainted saints

and confused Catholics

stunned by scandal,

lost its grip and all it's power.

Strip (1987)

O'Connell Street on an afternoon
you won't bump into a platoon
of soldiers or a tank or the muzzle of a gun,
or some Liverpudlian mother's son
in boots too big and heavy or his nineteen years
and no one fears the thoughts of being imprisoned.

But it isn't all that far away
that women rise to meet the day
that stretches into screaming
and if the memory of bars and steel
don't suffocate enough these women must be tough,
for they were in Maghaberry.

Security, protection, no adequate detection
were the reasons rhymed and years and years
it carried on when fear becomes a choking grip,
whens the sickening order filtered down
to strip.

These women bled with every passing day.

Now sorrow calls in darkness

of remembering

when the rain falls

outside the walls of Maghaberry.

Nakedness becomes a sea of shame

and no amount of washing

can remove the feel of filth

or print of fingers,

rancour lingers

long after any borders lifted.

Guns in Iowa

In April of 1999, thirteen kids in Columbine,
left pancakes and chocolate spread on breakfast tables
with absolutely no idea that by mid-morning
they would be splayed across a library floor,
skulls and ribs and limbs shot through with lead.
Thirteen futures butchered. Dead.

But in the state of Iowa blind people are not
to be denied their constitutional right to own a gun.
No rhyme or pun can make sense of a blind person
shooting mallard for recreation with an AK47.
Cedar County Sheriff Warren Wethington
said that it was, in law, a fact,
that a refusal for a permit,
would violate the Americans with Disabilities Act.

In 2012, December fourteen,
Adam Lanza killed twenty kids in between
the age of six and seven years old.
As his mother lay blue and cold,

in Sandy Hook Elementary school
nothing in the reading of a book,
could change the outcome of that winter's day.

The results of a report concluded that he had an
 "atypical preoccupation with violence and
easy access to deadly weapons"
which proved to be a "recipe for mass murder."
Six more were executed one by one
before he turned the gun to his own head
and damn near blew it off.
Total twenty-seven dead.

In Iowa Dubuque County, Sheriff Don Vrotsos
was in a minority when he stuck his head
above the parapet and said
out loud that he would be "disinclined
to issue a permit for a gun to someone who is blind."

In 2017, Vegas dead tolled fifty-eight,
the debate centred around the wisdom of bump stock.
The shock of America's deadliest massacre

ran down the strip as Stephen Paddock
steadied his grip to fire eleven hundred rounds
in quick succession before he, too,
blew his head off with his own weapon.
He had perfect sight, and exercised
his constitutional right to carry arms.

Just four years before, in Iowa,
Polk County officials admitted they've issued
weapons permits to three people
who can't legally drive and were unable
to read the applications, because
the nation's second amendment is very clear.

But it would appear not all of Iowa is united
in the wisdom of the decision.
"I'm not an expert in vision,"
said Delaware County Sheriff John LeClere,
"but if you see nothing but a blurry mass
in front of you, then I would say you
probably shouldn't be shooting something."

Excellent Horse Like Lady
(On reading the *Sunday Times* 09.06.19)

The phrase ran round and round in my head
on Sunday morning when I read
in the newspaper that Hong Song-ul
was not dead, or executed, as had been
believed in North Korea for some time,
but was now Kim Jong Un's official escort.

A pop star with a hit single that said
she was an *Excellent Horse Like Lady*.
In her own (I wonder) words, she sang
about being a virgin on a stallion
and having energy left after a full day's work
in the factory and I wondered,
what does a virgin on a stallion
do of an evening?

Apparently she is the first to leave for work
every morning, and has her name in the paper
for having skills like lightning,

"An award given to youths who live in flight,
to fight for the preservation
of the party era's teeming creation."
It's a very deep thought to have
with a bowl of cornflakes.

I think she must have some mad determination
or balls of steel to feel safe at the hands
or side of Kim Yong-un.
Apparently (it says) the virgin on the stallion
rides a horse given by the Dear Leader,
and me, a reader of the Sunday paper
eating toast could only feel inadequate
compared to the most enthusiastic virgin in the factory.

With perfect lips and hair and pastel
pink factory wear, singing with a smile
and hawking bolts of heavy cotton
without breaking out a sweat,
all tiredness she forgets when the whistle blows
and the factory gates spew out a hoard
of happy workers, laughing in the sun.

I got to wondering was she

the most deluded Popstar in the village,

or was she just the cleverest one?

But it seems this official escort of Kim Song un

feels no threat and is now celebrated as

number one North Korean First Lady,

and it's all a little shady though apparently she

is now no longer Hong Song-ul but is

the fully-fledged accompanying Dearest Leader's wife.

It's hard to know if she still believes that

she is an excellent horse like lady

virgin on a stallion

or is acting on a daily basis for survival

or for her very life.

H-Block March Drogheda 1981

Standing in the doorway of the bank,
porter
friend
affectionately respected
Father.
Chatting to the manager
in West Street.

They had left Belfast
the day before,
arriving now in growing numbers
carrying handmade coffins
clad in black
accompanied by
the local kids and usual hecklers.

"Shower of hooligans"
said my father
"Blocking the traffic"
said the manager.

She would have waved,

but her left hand carried

the homemade flag,

her right, her shopping basket

with floral umbrella in case of rain,

So my Auntie Bride shouted instead,

"Howya Eamon!"

Air Force Blue
(for Eamon Faulkner, in memoriam)

It's a rare and special gift to stay forever proud
of who you are and where it is you came from.
To live all your days near familiar roads and fields,
to know the branch of every tree
and the notes of every birdsong.

To embrace the new and yet hold dear
the memories of those you loved and knew,
who walked those same familiar roads before you.
To recall the ways that things were done
when you were young,
and to pass these stories down,
each one a special treasure,
one by one.

It's a rare and special man
who stays forever proud
of how his family grew,
we always knew how much you cherished

people close around you.
And it's not many men can
cut a dash in "Air force Blue."

It's a rare and special life
that's lived to the last, full and true.
And although your time with us is passed,
your legacy will live
as a man who had much to share
and much to give;
for that we say,
Cead Mile Buiochas.

Now I recognize the birdsong
and the branch of every tree.
Rest easy now, a legend to us
you will always be.

Charlie's Tree

He told me once, because I asked,
when I was small and he was planting dahlias,
"this is me and Charlie's tree, I have to keep it."
My mother wanted it cut down,
it blocked the light, she was insistent,
ranted and persisted.
He refused.

"I planted it with Charlie" he said softly,
"with cabbages and parsley in the springtime.
I watched them when he went away
and wrote to him fill him in on progress.
I didn't know where Peamount was,
I always thought he would be
coming home."

His voice was low and though I was
only six years old,
I knew that he was crying.
"Our cabbages are growing"

he said he wrote to Charlie,
resting on the shovel he remembered,
speaking soft to someone
in the rustling of the leaves
and in the wind song.

"Our cabbages are growing" he repeated,
as a stock still moment passed.
I watched him lower his head
to sink the shovel into pungent clay
upturning sleepy silken worms,
creating creature havoc
in the scattering of insects
Then he stopped,
and with him,
time.

Christmas Bikes Belfast 1990

Upper Canning Street, strictly Loyalist
Lower Canning Street, Republican
pulled down and being rebuilt
around a mural screaming "Tiger's Bay."

New city housing on a par with
any European suburb
built to house the four and five-year-old
wheelie kings and queens
who were showing me
their brand new Christmas Bikes.

North Queen Street metal cell
with six-inch lookout;
Bullet proof
Bomb proof
manned by snipers, highly trained
en-caged in rolls
of galvanized
barbed protection

from the four and five
year old wheelie kings
and wheelie queens,
showing me their
Christmas Bikes.

Paranoia in my Inbox

People are looking at your LinkedIn Profile!
So?
Do you want to know who they are?
Not really to be honest.
If you click on the link you can see who is looking.
No
If you click on the link you can upgrade your account
Then you will see who is looking at your profile
Why?
What?
Why would I need to see who is looking at my profile?
It will give you the edge on your competitors!
What competitors?
Just click on the link and take a month's trial, free.
No
Are you sure you don't want to find out who is looking
at your profile?
A month's trial is free of charge and you can change
your mind by unsubscribing.
I don't want to subscribe at all.

Lots of people use this facility and love it.

I don't want to know whose looking at my profile..

Will you click on the link?

Will you fuck off? You are making me paranoid!

But wait, are you SURE you want to leave this page?

Angelrest

(Holy Angels Plot, Drogheda 1999)

A people gathered, praying to
the soul of babies born
and lost in times of sadness.
Neighbour stood by neighbour standing
"I never knew, you as well, you hid it well"
and wept in private parochial sorrow.

So much time to try to find
a dank and shallow corner,
doused with rubble,
unmarked by any ordinated survey.
Cleaned up now, planted out,
marked with tiny steel framed cots,
silken flowers
and heart shaped headstones.

So much time and so much pain
to find a place to go to pray,
to talk, to cry

o try to say "we didn't know,
we, too, were lost."

A resting place knows little rest
as unsuspecting siblings
desecrate the graves
and smash the heart shaped headstones
on weekend drinking sprees
 and drug-fueled empty afternoons.

Under cold December moons
the mothers weep again
at broken alabaster.

The Pomegranate Tree

Abebi stopped the elders at her cabin door
baying for her girl child to be cut,
her husband cracked her face with calloused hands
but she slammed the flimsy plywood door shut.
She tore the skin from her uncle's forearm
when he tried to lift the child from a pallet bed,
her eyes red raw from crying, Abebi kicked
the still hot ashes from the grate into the faces
of the elders gathered at her garden gate.
The girl child asked "Mama, do they wait for me,
under the pomegranate tree?"

She screamed a string of litanies and hexes
as they waited with their dull edged rusty blade,
and other sister mothers carrying babies
gathered whispering softly in the midday shade,
then screeched their worries into the ink black night
that Abebi's actions with the girl child would invite
bad luck that her daughter should prepare
"for a life of barren spinster hood", Abebi didn't care.

Still she saw them gather round
when the dawn broke on the sun parched dusty ground.
The girl child asked "Mama, do they wait for me
under the pomegranate tree?"

The girl child gripped Abebi's skirts,
when she heard the drums and pleadings in the sun,
from the husband and the family
and the women of the village,
worried that the harvest tillage
would be failed and curses would be railed down
from angry Gods and prospective husbands.

The girl child said with silent eyes
 "I know what you have done for me
as I will do for mine, thank you Mama"
And the girl child asked
"Mama, do you think we are free?
no more the pomegranate tree?"

Harold in the Hospice

It made him tired to think about
putting in his teeth to bite an apple,
he didn't care if he took a pill or not,
(the pills they gave him now were for his bowels).
He wondered if the nurse had ever taken acid?
Did the Filipino orderly who always smiled
ever climb a tree at dawn high on coke
to see if he could hear electricity?
Did the doctor ever smoke a joint or eat a brownie
before the entrance exam for the civil service?
(no one was more surprised than Harold himself when
he got the job.)

Stamping forms in sandals and a cheesecloth shirt,
a head like Holyhead on Mondays
coked off his tits in Harcourt Street on Fridays,
getting locked into the downstairs bathroom
of Zhivago's (which was walled with mirrors)
sent him off the cliff edge.
They called it "a once off psychotic episode"

and locked him in St. Ita's for a week
(he remembered now being glad of the rest.)

Crawling into the luggage space
of an intercity bus leaving Dublin
to start a new life as a cobbler in Belfast,
was a great idea at the time,
fueled by drinking absinthe and smoking weed.
Freed by an overweight overwrought bus driver
Harold hitchhiked home from Drogheda at midnight.
(the damage to his lungs from diesel was severe.)

The hospice comfort dog was a cross between
a St. Bernard and a Labrador,
his eyes looked straight ahead
as bony yellowed hands and the almost dead
stroked his back and pulled his ears.
His name was "Titan" and he was commonly known
to have the patience of a saint.
Harold wondered if there were days
when Titan thought
"fuck this, the kip is full of sick people."

So he called the mongrel to his bedside

and in a last act of defiance

or enlightenment,

he slipped the dog a Valium.

Tinder Blunder

I think it might be time to tell this man I can't swim,
that I just wanted to be in the pool with him
as near to naked as a swimsuit with strong straps
and tummy control panel can make me.
Yellow rubber hat squeezing curled hair flat
and plastered to the side of my head,
I can understand now why he chose to ask me
last night, when we were in bed.

My chlorine coated eyes are shaded red
and bulging like contracted myxomatosis,
I wonder if I had not shaved my legs,
would he have seen my lines of navy varicosis?
I never realized that his left bollock is
twice the size of its brother,
and if there was ever anything other than
a fetish look to Speedos on a middle-aged man.

"I think I can!" I say
when he asks if I can swim away from the steps

to make room for his angry looking mother.

It's just as well the actual brother didn't come,
he is twice the size of him (Jim) but fat
and would also have a rubber hat
and I am just about maxed out
of mortified at this rate.
I thought it was a date,
not a family swimming medley
for mixed abilities and none,
on a Sunday morning.

I never thought when I swiped right,
that my inability to float would be an issue
"There is always one," says
the angry aged mother loudly,
flapping tissue paper arms
in the middle of the pool,
having swum past me like a jellied swan,
one rheumy eye looking at me, one looking *for* me.

I try to tread water

whilst simultaneously smiling

and worrying about sinking

-what the fuck was I thinking?

The Oxendales catalog described

a "discreet control panel" to flatten my belly,

what arrived was a polka-dot galvanized

contraption, breathing optional.

And it's true that on Tinder

I said that I liked swimming.

Synchronized to be exact,

but the simple fact I left out

was that it was of the Olympic variety

along with diving, and on the telly.

I should have said when he suggested

the Sunday morning meet,

"No, you are grand, go on ahead"

And stayed instead, with a made-up face

with dry and curly, shining hair

in a negligee for curvy older ladies,

like my profile picture, in bed.

Imbolg on the 29A
(Abbey Street to Baldoyle 2019)

Was St. Brigid Jesus's girlfriend Mammy?
-She was not son, sure we don't even know
who Jesus really was,
he could have been a leprechaun.

Or a woman Mammy?
-Don't say that! He was a man,
look at him in your book!
But he is wearing a dress and he has long hair Mammy

-I don't care, he was a man
and he lived in Nazareth
it says so in your book, look!
Anyway he has a beard.

If today is St. Brigid's day,
when is Jesus's Day Mammy?
-That's Christmas,
do you not know anything?

Where is he now?

Is he dead like they said Mammy?

Where is he now if he lives forever?

-He is everywhere and he can hear you

pestering me with all your questions.

If he is everywhere, where does he sleep Mammy?

-He never sleeps, I don't think.

I can see you winking, so you're lying Mammy

and that's a sin.

-Get your bag, put that can in the bin.

we are going to be late.

Mammy, is Jesus in Baldoyle Industrial Estate?

Just Desserts

A tin of peaches in a string bag
can do an awful lot of damage
to a bare knee
when suspended from the handlebars
of a moving bike.

If you add an east wind and heavy drizzle
and an anorak zip stuck halfway up
and halfway down, I am
an eight year old galloping hunchback
on a deserted country road
in Bettystown in 1972.

Birds Custard in a paper tin,
a box of Weetabix rub the skin
but don't split it open,
but the peaches,
oh the peaches
thump a dent until my knee bone screeches.

I gallop on through deathly hallows
in the company of squawking crows
and banshees screeching on electric cables,
strung across a dark gray silver sky
high above the winter blackened trees.

Skidding to a halt at the metal gate
The mother says I am too late,
dinner is nearly over
and would I ever stop bleeding
red drops of blood
on a newly washed floor
and to hang the string bag
on the back door

She said it would take too long
to make the custard
for the peaches
so she hopes that teaches
me "a bloody lesson."

Slap

I didn't see the slap coming
when it cracked my jaw and stung my skin.
I spilled the milk and watched helpless
as it bled white seeping stains on red Formica.

I couldn't understand,
all I did was say what you had said,
I thought that it was funny,
you said Granny was a "nosey bitch"
my face burned welt red.

I suppose you didn't realize that the granny
was standing at the back door,
and if I was wise
I would have kept my mouth shut
eyes fixed firmly on the kitchen floor.

But I was five and salt tears of shame
at some unfathomable misunderstanding
came thick and fast.

I tried to focus on the plate,
wells of water blurred my vision
as Angelus eighteen peals of purgatory
blared from the television.

In bed that night I dreamed of leaving,
my chest cracked sore
with heaving sobs,
but I didn't know
that you were grieving
for a dead baby.

Maybe if I'd known I might have stayed
until the cord was ready to be cut,
but at seventeen me and Janis Ian
went on a J One visa anywhere,
the slap still stinging on my face,
and pulled the back door
firmly,
finally
shut.

Blue Bells and High Horses

You have to leave the road to find a path,
carpeted with ferns and wild garlic,
and trees dressed in ivy swaddling
like lace on rough barks,
to find a lilac tinted pinafore around a trunk,
there you will see bluebells.

I wanted you to smell them too,
to remember how when we were young
we spent our hours talking to the ladybirds
and black soft caterpillars we called "God's Horses,"
splitting grass and counting smells
of honeysuckle and white-thorn blossoms
and heady gorse webbed in silk in early spring.

But here's the thing.
I forgot I came here in a temper
wanting to be on my own and left alone.
I stayed too long to find my way back to say
"It wasn't you, it was definitely me."

The road was empty,

you were gone.

And now it's hard to smell a bluebell

from a high horse.

A Great Man

(for Noel Delaney, in memoriam)

A simple man,
a kind man
a man whose mind was filled with poems
and possible ideas for fixing things
for making things,
for sowing things
for growing things.

A man with hands for any job
and a tool to do it with.
A busy man with things to do
places to go,
a man who knew his own mind
and didn't mind an argument,
But was at times
a quiet man.

A man who didn't like a fuss,

He was to us
a giant of a family man
with his own particular way
to wash the breakfast pot
before the start of day.

A man who leaves a legacy
of love and wisdom
Noel was, quite simply
A Great Man

Jax

You know the feeling when you want to go

and he's enrapt in stretching conversation,

you wait for hours

for pause or punctuation,

and when it comes

you say politely, if somewhat sharply

"Lookit, I have to go to the Jax."

Hoping something will hold it in 'till you find the loo,

you get there fit to burst and find

a bursting, red faced, cross legged queue

and so, we females exercise our amazing ability

not to burst.

By various positions of the legs,

crossed, knotted, shifting the weight

from one to the other

your bladder feels like Friesian's udder

when the milking machine breaks down

or there's a power cut.

In a brilliant attempt at mind over matter

you join in gossips delirious chatter

of fellow sufferers

until at last the toilet's empty-

rush in,

bang door,

knicks down

then you notice there is no lock,

O.K.

so you hold the door with one hand

stretched three inches longer than its normal length

and squat,

never, ever sit on the bowl!

Because your jeans were tight

and your position is unnaturally elongated

(on account of the door)

your aim deflects,

but you can't stop

four pints and two gins

the force of which is producing enough electricity

to do a seven pound wash on a short spin.

Then you begin,

the hapless search

under the bowl

and on the floor

and this is very difficult

when you are squatting with one hand

still holding the door.

Your heart sinks

when you realize there is none.

Not a square,

not a scrap

not even a cardboard holder

and so,

you almost dislocate your shoulder

as one hand *still* holding the door

you yank your jeans up and your knickers roll

into a rope around the tops of your legs

like they do when you go swimming

and don't dry yourself.

Electric shock of a wet waistband

means the shirt you so meticulously tucked in

when dressing will hopefully hang outside

and be long enough to prevent people guessing

if you've wet yourself.

Now, some of us have tried to make

a stand on this issue

and put off performance to march defiantly to the bar

to ask for some toilet tissue.

"Certainly Madam" the bar man says,

"will you be wanting it with ice and lemon?"

as he and his cronies piss themselves laughing

if you'll pardon the pun

And he hands you a catering bale of Andrex.

So you take the rolls and cross the room

trying to look nonchalantly cool

And feeling like an eejit

Until you reach it

Ladies loo

Complete with queue

Then it's you

And then you're in

Bang the door

knicks down, arm out

paper ready

but

you

can't

go.

Nothing.

Not a drop.

Not a trickle.

Cold sweat,

and then a lone pathetic dribble

after all that.

When this happened to me

I heard a woman next door

grumble and fumble and feel on the floor.

"Do you want paper?" I shouted

my voice getting higher

"Paper?" she shouted

"I need a fucking hair dryer!"

Now I know that paper is made from trees

and people are genuinely worried

about the slaughter of the tropics

which is affecting the ozone

and messing up the weather,

but if this happens to you

I would humbly suggest

you use half a roll

for spite and badness

and put a wad inside your pocket

in case you get caught short on the way home.

So you might as well lash back the pints

and drown in the gin

with the jax in the pub

a woman can't win.

Spatchcock Chicken

Eight years after my second child

in a hot flush or after a flash decision
I decided to have the coil removed,
having been assured by the newly qualified
balding gynaecologist who inserted it
that it would be a simple procedure
when the time came that it was no longer needed.

So I booked an appointment with my female doctor
and asked her to retrieve it.
Unconcerned that in the intervening years
bush went out of fashion, it never entered
my head to have the hairs on my lady garden
ripped off with hot wax to maximize my sex appeal.

She smiled behind the mask
when I revealed my natural state,
and she said of late full bushes were rare
but my blushes were for my assumed position,

soles together,
spatchcocked chicken.

She found it hard to keep a steady hand and I knew
if I didn't have my tonsils out when I was twenty-two,
I would have thought she was going to remove them
there and then by the wrong avenue.
I knew that she was struggling
as I was juggling with the wisdom of the idea
of a new baby and an eight year old.
My blood ran cold when her head
appeared above the hedgerow
with a look of worry
"I am sorry, Anne" she said as she held aloft
a piece of blue nylon thread.
"This just came off. You will have to go to A&E"

"Are you fucking kidding me?"
I know was not language
I should probably use to a qualified physician
but I had been over forty minutes by then
in the spatchcock position.

I decided I would not be defeated and was
definitely not going to be cheated
out of my ability to conceive,
so I knew the very person who might
retrieve the coil without a fuss…
the original balding gynaecologist,

I raced to his surgery and as I entered
I saw a sign that read "Driving Test Center."
So I Googled him and with a bit of digging
traced his new premises
to a clinic over a chemists shop in Balbriggan.

"You might not remember me" I said
to his now perfectly smooth completely bald head.
"You put a coil in eight years ago
so I was hoping you could take it out."
If he recognized me from where he was standing
I couldn't say, but I wanted so badly to have
the thing removed that I assumed the position,
spatchcock chicken
and he preceded to try to locate the device.

After thirty minutes on his advice
I tried to think of something happy,
so I looked out the window
of his upstairs clinic at the sky,
straight into the faces of the passengers
on the top deck of the 191,
Dublin to Balbriggan bus
which was passing by
slowly before stopping for a red light

"There should be a piece of blue nylon string"
he said, and by now his head was glowing.
"I know the other doctor took it" I replied
Trying not to make eye contact
with the passengers inside the bus.
He dug a bit deeper and if I wasn't already
lying down I would have fainted
From sheer mortification.
Suddenly he held up his tongs
and shouted "Here it is!"
He was all biz, like he found his true vocation.
I tried to be happy on the way home

sitting with some difficulty

on a ring of foam and giant night-time things

with wings in my knicks.

Just for kicks I asked the hubby

if he still really wanted another baby.

His face had that panic-stricken look

that knows the wrong answer could be fatal

So he said "maybe?"......

He looked a bit stricken

so I made the decision, our lot is our lot.

"Well we're not" I announced.

"And another new rule is no matter

how tender the BBQ or finger licking,

we will *never* again eat a spatchcock chicken!"

A Very Zoom Affair
(for the poet and activist Margaret O'Regan)

She wished she had thought to put nicer dress on
as she clicked on Zoom,
she had taken a YouTube class on how to minimize
the glare on your glasses from your laptop,
then read a poem about how she enjoyed being alone
but also loved meeting new people
and how she hated sheeple
and how individuality was her thing.

He read about what he had to bring
to a new relationship.
He took down the Man Utd poster from the wall
of his son's bedroom where he did the calls
and replaced it with a Mogdialani print,
then read a poem about still having a spring in his step
and a zing in his homemade Covid margaritas.

She read in front of her kitchen window
with her pots of basil and mint

complementing the blue of her new top,

he could not stop reading about when he travelled

as a young man and how aging had made him wiser

and more open to his feminine side.

She told her friends that

from what she could see he was a big ride.

She started wearing perfume

to the online open mic nights,

dimming the lights so that her wrinkles were depleted.

He read about how proud he was that he had

completed a degree by night, and how it was the right

of everybody-woman or man to an education.

She read about how she loved the grounds of Trinity

College in the winter.

He read about how he didn't even feel the splinter

in his heart now that his partner had moved on

and how he longed for a relationship

with a woman of culture.

She read about a previous relationship
with an energy vulture
and how she now embraced the empty nest.

He read about how he had used yoga
to lay all his demons to rest.
She read about shopping online
and how not all bullets need guns.
He read about using puns to deliver a punch in a poem.
She read about nights when she would be alone.
He read about being on his own in his king-size bed.
She dreamed of his words going around in her head.
He wished to fuck the barbers would open.
She read about coping without getting
her highlights done and how she was
actually very happy to be grey.

The day she knew the jig was up
was when she wore suspenders on the open mic
under her leggings and used her contact lenses
to get rid of the glare,
when into the view of the screen

came her husband's hand,

wrapped around a cup of coffee

his wedding band glinting in the sun

from the kitchen window.

"That's for yourself doing the poetry"

the husband said,

her face flushed fire engine red.

She composed herself and read about ships in the night.

He read about ships that had just fucking sailed.

She wailed loudly off camera

that she was only having a bit of fun

and wasn't she entitled to just one little bit

of the house to herself.

He decided NOT to read at the next open mic

but appeared on the call beside a photo

of him, the wife, and a Christmas elf,

his copy of Ulysses strategically placed

on a hastily erected IKEA shelf.

Codladh Sámh (lyrics for a ballad)

I remember how the Samhain moon
on inky waters shone.
I watched you push the currach out
that bore our stillborn son.
Wrapped in the wedding dress you wore
when first you came to me,
when we wed with bands of silken thread
beneath a willow tree.

Codladh sámh a stoir, Codladh sámh a stoir
Codladh sámh a stoir, Mo Chroí
Sleep well my love, sleep well my love
Till I come to comfort thee.

I called you from the towering cliff
four seasons to the day.
No comfort for your aching heart
did I have words to say.
The Samhain moon and howling wind
my words brought back to me,

a halo from your petticoat sank deep into the sea.

Codladh sámh a stoir, Codladh sámh a stoir
Codladh sámh a stoir, Mo Chroí
Sleep well my love, sleep well my love
Till l come to comfort thee.

Eight moons passed,
your body found
washed up along the quay.
Your petticoats now seaweed trails
your eyes no longer see.
Your song my heart will always keep
until I come to thee,
my wife and child, ten fathoms deep
I hear you calling me.

Codladh sámh a stoir, Codladh sámh a stoir
Codladh sámh a stoir, Mo Chroí
Sleep well my love, sleep well my love
Till I come to comfort thee.

I cannot, yet, to water's edge
when Samhain's moon shines on.
For when I do, to be with you
my wife, my still born son.
My pockets filled with polished stones
I know that we will be,
united once again my love
beneath the Samhain sea.

Codladh sámh a stoir, Codladh sámh a stoir
Codladh sámh a stoir, Mo Chroí
Sleep well my love, sleep well my love
Till I come to comfort thee.

One Piece Missing (A poem in the pandemic)

She built a bird feeder, I made a jigsaw
and over weeks and days we found our ways
to be together, a trial run at empty nest syndrome.

It's gone pretty well so far,
except for one or two minor details;
the cat eyeballs the pigeons
when they attempt to feed,
and my jigsaw has one piece missing.

What are the chances that the Christmas present
that lived for months under the couch
and on the floor, and was short listed
at one stage by the front door for the S.V.P.
would have a piece gone A.W.O.L.?
One in a thousand actually.

The bird-feeder is full of nuts and seeds.
The pigeons make it to the path outside the window,

one small step is all it takes to make the balcony,
one small piece is all it takes to make the jigsaw.
A piece I fear long since consumed
by the settee or the hoover or the same cat
who dares the pigeons to take a chance.

This might be our last dance
before the world returns to being busy
and important and time is measured
again by productivity, not pleasure.

When the world and we look back
at how we spent our hours and days,
and try to count the ways we used
to make something of the lock-down,
I will smile at black and white and brown
pieces of a puzzle made without hurry
or a flurry of activity.

I hope that I would not forget
how precious was the time we spent.
In future days when reminiscing,

I will remember the nine hundred
and ninety nine pieces that were there,
not the one piece missing.

Other titles by Seabhac Publishing:

Songs from the Worn Hole 2016 by Muddy D Norman

Whale Bones 2019 by Muddy D Norman

The Holding Cell 2020 by Jo Hinch

For more information email seabhac@gmail.com

Printed in Poland
by Amazon Fulfillment
Poland Sp. z o.o., Wrocław

90831485R00073